There Is a Horse in Me

poems by

Patricia Starek

Finishing Line Press
Georgetown, Kentucky

There Is a Horse in Me

For my mom, Anne Little Scaff: you gave me my words

For Isaiah and Ellis Harrison: you gave me them back

ACKNOWLEDGMENTS

Some of these poems were previously published in *Mom Egg Review, Fall Lines—A
Literacy Convergence* and featured on WNYC.

Thank you, Glenis Redmond, you have been an unflappable friend, trusted mentor,
Auntie to my sons and creative inspiration. Your belief in me and my words and your
gentle push made this book a reality.

Thank you, Cheryl Boyce-Taylor, from the moment I stepped into your space, you
have provided joy and friendship and mentorship. We cherish you Tanty Cheryl.

Thank you, Mom, you are the one who introduced me to the love of words and made
sure we used them with integrity.

Thank you, Mrs. Brooks at Phillips Jr. High School you found my first poem,
crumpled in the back of a desk and called me in to check on my heart and tell me
that I could write.

Thank to my husband, Derik Harrison. You have delighted in words with me over the
years. You also dared me to step up. And to my boys, Isaiah and Ellis, without you,
this book would not be.

Special Thanks to Sandor Hartung, the artist whose lithograph is the cover art. I met
you in the spring of my youth so many years ago, purchased your print and covet it.
Grateful to celebrate your creative gifts here. hartungsandor.hu

Publisher: Leah Huete de Maines
Editor: Christen Kincaid
Cover Art: Sandor Hartung, Lithograph, *Sky Rider*
Author Photo: Patricia Starek
Cover Design: Elizabeth Maines McCleavy

Order online: www.finishinglinepress.com
also available on amazon.com

Author inquiries and mail orders:
Finishing Line Press
PO Box 1626
Georgetown, Kentucky 40324
USA

Contents

there is a horse in me

there is a horse in me
that runs
there is

there is a horse
that knows
knows my kin in the dark
blood recognized by breath

there is a horse
that thunders across space
powerful thighs
huge lungs
synchronize
soar

there is a horse in me
that knows rest
exhalation
there is

there is a horse in me
scared of bridges
spooked by flickering branches
moving cars

a horse in me
with the softest ears
360 surround sound

a horse in me
bridled
saddled
blinded
central park denizens
metal shoe on concrete screaming streets
spurs into hide
buckaroo they ride
stabled
always separated from child

there is
there is a horse in me
there is

carousel

your body shakes
as we approach
The Carousel
Brooklyn
blue slashes of sky
interrupted by
treasured Brooklyn trees
broccoli trees
you call them

the music
the carousel music
wailing joyful agony
clowns lament
scary cacophony

you shake
an ice cream
we'll have an ice cream first
settle in observe
we buy an Eskimo bar
you rebel
no ice cream bar
this is not the soft ice cream
you have only recently come to love
your small tongue
dances on the soft serve

I explain
it's ice cream in a cookie
"No ice cream in a cookie"
you scream
you flat out fall out

so we watch
carved ponies
stoic lion
you ready?
"yes"
"yep"

you we stand in line
a dollar fifty later
we mount the 92-year-old
wooden platform
and you protest
no pony no pony
shaking resisting
I eye the stationary pony
place you on
precarious climb on back

other toddlers
shimmy and shake

the bell clangs
announcing impending
movement
and you're not having it

we slide off
slide into sleigh
mercifully one horse back
the conductor cranks up the wheel
around you go

you fold into my chest
three horses bob up and down
behind us
teeth barred for many hostage years
you stare
stunned
and fold your head outward
to the snatches of sky
smiling parents
waving at their progeny

you are still
not very 2-year-old boy still
the carousel careens
I do not remember this speed

and I weep
so easily
already nostalgic for this moment
safe scary moment
my chest is enough
absolute anchor

ride winds down
you lift your head
quietly proclaim
I like it
pony mama I like it

it's only out from here
my sweet sweet boy
afraid for what you'll fear
and that which draws you near

pay attention

i pay attention

attention to august
heirloom juicy salted
tomato

cool sheets
on bare legs

sensual circle
of sleeping cat

roar of the Atlantic

breath yours

I pay attention
to new worry lines
etched into dear
friend's face

attention to
honest eyes
dismissive backs

bedrock words
mudslides

condemned souls
mangy animals

rivers and blood

changing skies

strong patient trees

symphony of hearts
orchestrating my actions

poverty and privilege
the pop of pistachio

fresh limes salt and war

I pay attention

attention to
cumulus clouds
goddamn have
you looked at a
cumulus cloud
recently

breath
yours
marrying
mine
as we move
into mercurial
night

Glass Travels

Once upon a time
Before I was a married
Woman

I bought these
In San Miguel de Allende
2,484 miles from home

Off the Zocalo
Under a blue sky
Miles from home

Once upon a time
I drove to San Miguel
From Brooklyn

With dearest
Friend
Alicia

Releasing this dear
From the grind
The heartbreak
The ugly
Of this apple
To the heart
The ease
The beauty of
Mexico

We drove from here
To there
Stayed in glorious
Historical hotels
Wrote my fiancé letters on
Hotel stationary all along the way

Me in between the then and the now
Punctuated by
Deep silence

Deep laughter
Conversation only had between trusted friends

I practiced my bad Spanish

With tapes (tapes!)
Along the way
We ate local food
Read our Animal Cards
At the border
Between here and there

Dressed like men
To appease
Her worried Mama
At 4am
Crossed the border in Laredo
Nervous as shit

Crossed giddy
1st meal
Eaten after we impulsively drove way up a dirt
Road to an old Silver mining town
A beautiful Italian meal
Of a courtyard
Served by a beautiful hip Italian woman

Stereotypes melting
Like the snow
Under salt
On my walk
Right now

This trip
A parenthesis
Between the then and the now
Homage to me
Wandering ways
To my
Once Upon a time

I bought my mother
Modern Czech crystal
Home in a backpack
Unscathed
Soon I'd be wed
Soon I'd be pregnant
With my deep and kind boy
Soon I'd be a
New me
So today
I will fill these
Beautiful handblown
Glasses
With smoky frosty
Tequila
and dream

dream about the next
once upon a time

out in the world
backpack opened to the
treasure adventure
collecting glass
confident humbled hopeful
in the safe passage home

The Weight
(Third Child)

The air
The always breathes
Words
Words into me

The ground
These days
The ground is so heavy
Duty Stagnates

Loss and change `
all around
The weight of loss
Loss does not wait for you

Father is there
Then not
Left with the weight of memory

Colleague, beloved, brilliant is there
Then not
Left with the weight of the torch

Dear Friend's son is there
Then not
Left with weight of a Mother's grief
The weight of legacy

My small child
a whirling dervish of words
His breath
His frame
Fiercely alive with every question
He is compact joy with the drive of Zeus
Tiny tincture of supreme curiosity

Exhausts parents
Call him he mayor

My older child
Dreamer
Friend to All
Joy on the field
Brown boy limbs grow long
Questions swirl

Natural activist
The horror of 2016
The horror of history
Questions swirl
The agony of sending my long brown boy into the world
Unsafe world
Will the world hold him close
Confirm his life matters

Corporate machine
Fires the ultimate nasty woman
Leaves us breathless
Calculated greed
Where do I belong

The weight of the night
Sleep sleep as soon as allowed
Insomnia swirls neck jaw groan
Numbers and un-memorized frozen lines

Cancer
Mercurial serpent
Sits on the steps

Paying attention to it all
Pay attention to nothing
A vacuum

And so I consume

Consume
Dirty food
Registers
Like Atlantic City

Consume the screen
Make America Great Again
Consume the hate
The disbelief
Black hole of loss

Cheez It's down the gullet
Wine
Unhappy elixir

Poured too easily
Poured Alone

3rd child of anxiety
3rd child of grief
30 pounds
30 pounds!

Weight of loss
Weight of duty
Weight waiting on the serpent
Growth memory
Night   White hate
Greed
Weight of belonging
Weight of US

I did not write that poem

thought about it
last year

that poem about his

high C
sweet soprano
secret voice

Just one year ago

perfect pitch
my dad proclaimed

on the precipice
between there and
now

still a boy
in the next room

singing
hitting
the highest bell notes
free

I did not write that poem

and now they are gone

my boy is gone
Into the deep

notes of himself
bass
baritone
still unknown

he's gone
Into the deep

finding his range

Four and a Half Spins
—for Ellis

he is perfectly four and a half
this unexpected boy
this boy five years in the making
complete surprise
no mistake
born with eyes wide open
6 hours old
In Tanty Cheryl's lap
staring
anointed a wordsmith
deep brown
eyes cut to the center
dark brown light
and now at four and a half
he slows this lumbering earth
quiets anxious chaos
my spinny brain
tiny bodhisattva
he spins
claps
eyebrows raised
discerning
this deep joyful sprite
constant questions
constant breath
the agency of a river
he knows
has always known how and where to flow
has a jaunty little skip
cheers when I come home
cheers for small joy
He
Is
Just
So
Here
I hold fast to his exuberance

Learning to Ride

My tightly wrought boy

He's learning
To balance
It's hard
Does not want to fall
To fail
Soon
Will be up against that
Terrifying
Magic moment

He will have to let go

On Leaving

Hard to
Leave the heart
Big heart of 2-year-old wide open
Big head of 8-year-old finding
His heart in the world

Taxi too early
Little one on my leg
Frantic I want mommy
Big one worries about Skype
How are we going to connect

Zipper is fucking stuck
The taxi is there
Light low in the sky
Heart in feet

Every Day All The Time

Parenting From a Plane
Trying to do it all
Growing up a kid in NYC

The meeting had not been great
Well parts were invigorating
Right people assembled
Right conversation
Wrong preparation

Walking onto the plane
beating myself up
Seated next to a "nice" seeming woman
who is clearly traveling for work as well

From afar I remember that our
sitter/Uber driver pick up for a pre-teen in Brooklyn
cannot pick up our 11-year-old for soccer
Call husband who is luckily home to remind him to
pick-up said 11-year-old from the library
I wake him from a nap
He will pick him up
He thinks practice starts at 5:30
It starts at 4:30
It's 4:35

and he will learn with the reading of this piece that I am fiercely
annoyed that he does not have the soccer schedule on lock

Back to the plane
Text and Calls
11-year-old NOT at the library
He is NOT at the playground
He is NO WHERE TO BE FOUND
Texts fly
More calls made
illegally while pulling back from the gate
pissing off flight attendant
Should I post "Missing 11-year-old on FB?"

I am crying in the airplane window
simultaneously aware of the nice woman next to me
She reminds me we can text while flying Delta

I tell one of my mommy friends Sally that this will be the worst
flight of my life

Husband still can't find him
We are closing in on an hour and the other one must be picked up
from afterschool

My brain is awash with unmentionable disasters

You suck as a parent
You created no back-up plan
Why don't you have tracking turned on his phone
Remember he left it at home fully charged

and then
phone rings

Zay
incoming call

relief like water
pours all over me

He is Home
He walked home
1.5 miles through the streets of Brooklyn
Walked home
Got there
Bff got word of his missing status through the panic chains and
called him on his PS4
"Yo, your mom is freaking out, call her"

He does
Mom, are you crying?
Why?
and I breath hearing his breath

Sweet deep easy
first child of mine

He did it
He had a plan
He did it right
He did exactly the right thing

We hang up
my nice neighbor turns to me
exhales

she says she has been crying a little bit with me too

and we do
What really only women can
bond quickly
over shared struggle
and airplane wine
the dramas
the choices
we make every day

Each choice
a weight
what is right
right for me
my kids
my family
the greater good

Every Day
All the time

Sad

(Pandemic Blues and More)

I am so sad
Like all over body sad
Drink in the middle of the day
Hard to see a way out
Want to make it better but can't
I can't shake the sad

Loss upon loss
She does not need any more loss
She's had her share of loss
Can't make sense of the loss
Rage at the loss

Hard to be grateful for what you have
Breath shallow
Horrible void sad
Up all night
Motherless child
This just fucking sucks

sad

Some people make babies, and it makes them sad
Some people can't make babies and it makes them sad

Miscarriage
A strange word
She carried with all she had
All her hope
All her potions and dreams and vitamins and following the doctors
and the hive mind's orders
She carried so much hope
She wanted that baby
She wanted that baby so much sad

Sad because
The world is on fire
The basements are filled with water
People cling to airplane tires as they take off

And vitriol is being handed out like straws at the bodega
All that sad

Stones on my chest
She carried that baby
And wanted her so much

Because I remember
Her
Because I remember
Him

You do too
Right?

I am so sad
Like all over body sad
Drink in the middle of the day
Hard to see a way out
Want to make it better but can't
Damn I'm sad
So sad

Simple Request

The request was simple
Can my child come say hello to your child?
With appropriate social distance of course

It has been 8 weeks since this 7-year-old has seen a friend in the flesh

Yes, come by on your walk
He would love that

And he waited
With rapt breath
Stood on the couch staring down the road
Waiting for his friend to arrive

Within minutes
There were requests for scooters
Running around the block
Sleeves were torn
Masks were off
Bubbles in the air
Nerf guns
Soccer balls
Laughter

Sweet laughter

His mom, masked
Looked at me
She and I
Still 12 to 20 feet away
Is this ok?
Should we be doing this

Joy feels scary
Play
The work of childhood
Denied

After 15 or so jubilant minutes
We cut it off

I'm sorry, she said
You're gonna have to disinfect it all

My child, the happiest he's been in days
Rushed into house to wash his hands

Leaning into the Solstice

Leaning into the Solstice
Long morning light on my shoulders

Like a balm like a bath
On a sad morning

Heading into the long night
Nourished by the sun

Permission to hibernate
Permission to grieve

This house is uneasy

It swallows me in the night
Nestled in clouds of comforters
Legions of cats
The light grows short and I retreat
Into books a bed a prayer
I am a river damned

I want coze
I want ease
I want counterspace clear
Clear for the recipe
Clear for the poem
Clear for the tray
For tea and biscuits
With surprise guest friend

I want that desk that
Beckons my name
Sit at this wooden temple
And polish the truth

My floors want Persian carpets
Ancient red
Burnished blue
Persian carpet
Upon parquet floor
Floor broad for
Frolicking for
Rolling around with baby

I want a bed big
Big for cats and lover
And wonder of baby
Big temple of family

I want music in the walls
And strangely it is opera
It is big classical big tenor voices
I want easy order
An open door

Welcome mat
Energy and solace

Somebody hijacked my home

The kitchen is ready for a meal
The bath a hot spring

I want my Godmother's grace
Easy as she opens her table

Sometimes I am uneasy explosion
I am still 10 stuffing the closet shut full so many ball in the air
And hands tied behind the back erratic snake

Somebody hijacked my home

Sometimes I am river
Sometimes there are candles
6 course meals
Oils herbs and community glasses
Loud loud loud
Simple sum hands held

Tonight I will be the river
I'll hijack it back
Invite chaos over
Giver her a seat at the table
Break open a beer
Broker a deal
Make this house a home

It is Saturday night, and I am Crying in the Laundry Mat

What has my life come to
Spin cycles

It started out poorly
As I parked
He laid on the horn
I got out of the car, and he yelled
Ruddy nosed white man in the passenger seat
"You're blocking me in!"
Sir, I said, "I have a camera, I was not going to hit you/you have three
feet in between us"
him "You're boxing me in"
I tell him we can be civil about this
He will not meet my gaze
I move forward a bit moving slightly into the NO Parking anytime zone
Tears spring to my eyes
I go to the meter to pay, and he has about 6 feet behind him
I clearly know not what exactly is boxing this man in

On to the washing
Two full bags of the big throw rugs the new washable rug (that has
emboldened me to get a light rug in my smallish NYC space) and
linens
Too much for the home machine
My sister and partner crossing the country tomorrow
Their arrival has thrown me into a frenzy of washing and cleaning and
down on my knees scrubbing corners
They are tidier than me

In goes the covering for the little ones old changing pad cover
He's 9 now will not be needing that anymore (gulp)
In goes the Superman blanket Nana made Zay when he was little
Long overdue for the spin cycle (he's taller than me now)
In goes my grandmother's linen tablecloth/traveled her from Iran to
her table and my aunt's
table and now my table and it is stained, and I am hoping OxiClean can
bring my past back to the table. Half of my heritage
Half of my longing.
In it goes

The little Farsi speaking boy holds on to the huge front loader washer
and vocalizes with the machine as it spins and vibrates
He is thrilled
He so little it almost looks like the machine will lift him right into
atmosphere
His brother rides around the laundry mat on a hoverboard
A married couple flow back and forth between English and a language
I do not recognize are still clearly love with each other and freely flirt in
a lovely way
I watch them covertly

The rugs spin

I have 20 minutes
I decide to go the bar next door
This feels a little like a Saturday Night Thing to do
Sit outside
Next to the subway platform
Drink a glass of rose
With a random collection of solo neighbors
It's a little too breezy
The woman in front of me takes a shot with the proprietor
And soon after tumbles out onto the sidewalk after tripping over a
cinder block
And its awkward
And we jump up to help her
And her torso is exposed
And I feel embarrassed for her
I have to return to the linens

it's too breezy
My husband away for work
I've left my children home to be parented by small screens
My closest NYC friends have all left the city
I am alone

Transfer to the dryer
Hold the sheets to the nose
Take in their freshness
Watch them tumble

Soon I pull my grandmother's tablecloth out of the dryer
In an instant
I am gutted
How many times did I sit at her table?
Her table making was epic
We waited to eat all day when we were invited
2nds and 3rds not optional
As soon as we entered
She urged us to the table
Come Children Eat

pojďte jíst dět

she so far away from home
in humid North Carolina
The only Grandma I came to know

And I turn my back to the cute flirty couple
And the tears flow
As I stare at the dryer

Stream down my cheeks
Easy
Welcome
And yet I hide them
In the laundry mat

On this Saturday night of longing

And so we gather

18 months
So much lost
Disconnected from loved ones

And now we discover
What is found

We cross the country
Cross the street

To gather again

We longed for communion
Baked bread
Dressed for the camera

Contemplated

What do we bring to the table?

Who are we
Outside of these walls?

And so, we gather

I'll bring Grannie's mac and cheese
And my newfound
Roasted cranberry pineapple salsa

What will you bring?

How about what's on your mind?
Your heart

And we will gather
The table dressed in its finest

Grateful we gather

Finding what we lost
What is found

Spring   This Year

each year
these tiny botanical explosions
steal my breath

this year they
bring me to tears

for two years
our collective breath
held
feared
contracted
all of us on God Damn Mute

and there they are
regular
expected
astonishing
glorious

they arrive
with all the wisdom
all the moxie
of the dormant branch

deep brown
unadorned
waiting
ready to explode
to return
to delight

Sweet Mouth
—Dedicated to my mouth and Dr. Eric Steinbach, DDS

I had forsaken you
Forgot you

    denied
No ~~ignored~~

Even at night
After night

There was that dull ache
That low throb

I decided the remedy
Worse than
The thing

And I went on
About my business

All wrapped up in
Mommy duty
The Grind

The getting up
The getting out
The picking them up
The going home
And what's for Goddamned dinner

And I used you
All the damn time

Food in
Precious air

Deep laughter
Head thrown back
In laughter

Roaring from my mouth
Pretty words

Words shared in confidence
And the "mmm hmms" and

"yes I know" and "wow, that must have been hard"
Only passed between
Cherished friends

And my lips
On my sweet baby's head
My lovers neck

And spread wide
In spontaneous
Fireworks
Grateful
Smile

And them one of those
Damn
Day Time Doctors
Talked about
Plaque on your heart
Plaque on your teeth
Plaque in your head

And you cracked
Baby cavity fell into you

You invited me
Demanded

Care

Reverence for you
Sweet mouth

So I found the best
The hip tattooed Brooklyn DDS
With candles in the bathroom
Spa music in the walls
An art major no less

and tended to the neglect
he so good I wrote this poem while he drilled and tended to my words
my air
my heart
this life
this wonder
thank you, sweet mouth

North Carolina Native and Brooklyn denizen, **Patricia Starek**, marries two passions: teaching and writing. Her career as a poet began quietly as a teenager navigating change and weaving her reality into metaphor. In 1996, she moved loudly into the slam arena as a member of the Asheville, NC slam team. Higher education brought her to New York City, and she has since performed through the city, across the United States and internationally. She holds a master's in special education from Bank Street College of Education and taught in the NYC public schools dedicating her professional work to those locked out of the magic of words.

She's performed with award winning poet, Glenis Redmond in a two woman show called *Stepsisters, a Two Women Dialogue on Women, Race and Friendship.* She's recorded a CD called *Shh!!* and has been most recently published in the *Mom Egg Review, Fall Lines*—a literacy convergence and featured on WNYC during National Poetry month. She has authored several poems honoring teachers that have become animated works and published by Houghton Mifflin Harcourt. She's obsessed with vocabulary.

Life feeds her poetry and poetry feeds her spirit. She lives in Brooklyn with her husband the two sons.